# The Solar System

HOWARD K. TRAMMEL

**Children's Press®**
An Imprint of Scholastic Inc.
New York  Toronto  London  Auckland  Sydney
Mexico City  New Delhi  Hong Kong
Danbury, Connecticut

**Content Consultant**
Noreen Grice
Astronomer
President, You Can Do Astronomy, LLC.
www.youcandoastronomy.com

Library of Congress Cataloging-in-Publication Data

Trammel, Howard K., 1957-
 The Solar System / by Howard K. Trammel.
   p. cm.—(A true book)
  Includes index.
   ISBN-13: 978-0-531-16898-1 (lib. bdg.)     978-0-531-22805-0 (pbk.)
   ISBN-10: 0-531-16898-0 (lib. bdg.)     0-531-22805-3 (pbk.)

1. Solar system—Juvenile literature.  I. Title. II. Series.

QB501.3.T73 2010
523.2—dc22          2008049376

1 2 3 4 5 6 7 8 9 10 R 19 18 17 16 15 14 13 12 11 10          62

# Find the Truth!

**Everything** you are about to read is true *except* for one of the sentences on this page.

Which one is **TRUE**?

**T or F**   The Sun is the largest object in our solar system.

**T or F**   Saturn is the only planet with rings.

Find the answers in this book.

# Contents

*Galileo Orbiter* approaching Jupiter

4

Without the Sun there would be no life on Earth.

THE **BIG** TRUTH!

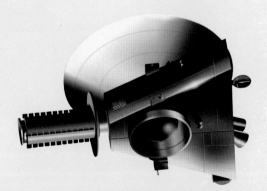

*New Horizons* spacecraft

Planet Earth is part of the solar system.
The solar system is located in a galaxy
called the Milky Way. The Milky Way is
one of billions of galaxies in the universe.

# CHAPTER 1

# Welcome to the Solar System

 Our solar system formed 4.6 billion years ago.

Thousands of years ago, people thought that Earth was the center of the universe. But now we know that's not true. Our planet is one part of our solar system. The solar system is made up of everything in space that travels around our Sun.

# Know the Solar System

Along with the Sun, eight planets make up our solar system. These planets are very different from each other. Some are so big that Earth would disappear in one of their storm clouds. There are planets with rings of ice and dozens of moons.

**The Sun is the closest star to Earth. It is 93 million miles (150 million kilometers) away from our planet.**

Mercury

Venus

Earth

Mars

Sun

Jupiter

But planets aren't the only objects in the solar system. **Comets** leave tails of glowing gas for millions of miles. The moon and tiny **meteoroids** light up our sky. There is still much to discover about our solar system.

How to remember the order of the planets: My Very Excellent Mom Just Served Us Noodles.

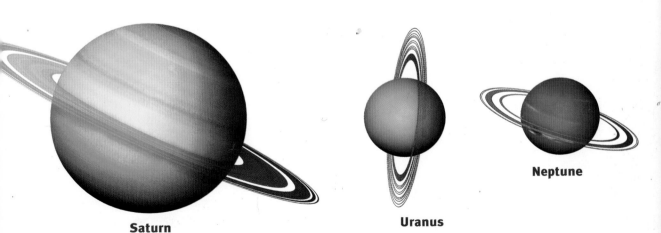

Saturn

Uranus

Neptune

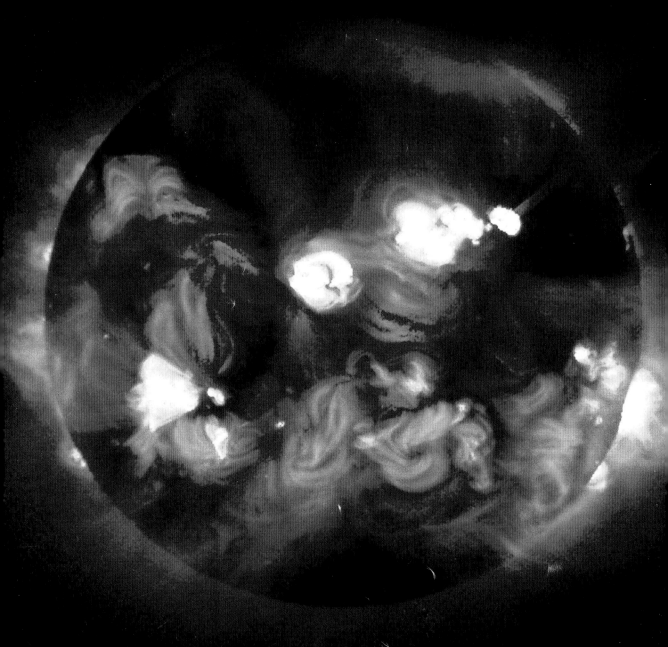

The Sun's surface is almost 10,000 °F (5,500 °C).

# CHAPTER 2

# The Sun

The most important part of the solar system is the Sun. The Sun is a star that gives off light. It's also much bigger than anything else in the solar system. The Sun makes up 99 percent of everything in the solar system. One million Earths could fit inside the Sun. The Sun's **gravity** is why the solar system stays together.

It takes more than 8 minutes for the Sun's light to reach Earth.

The sky appears orange at sunset and sunrise because the Sun is very low in the horizon. The sunlight is scattered by dust particles in the air.

# Force of Nature

Gravity is an invisible force that pulls one object toward another object. The larger an object is, the stronger its gravity. When you jump, you fall to Earth because its gravity pulls on you.

The Sun's gravity keeps the planets and other solar system objects traveling in **orbits** around it. All objects in the solar system are affected by the Sun's gravity. Planets also have gravity which keeps smaller objects, such as moons, in orbit around them.

# In Orbit

Each planet in our solar system travels around the Sun at a different speed. At the same time a planet orbits the Sun, it spins like a top. This spinning is why there's night and day on planets. The Sun can also affect a planet's temperature. Mercury is very hot since it's close to the Sun. But Neptune is so far away from the Sun that it's nearly frozen.

## Length of Orbit Around the Sun

| Planet | Earth Days |
|---|---|
| Mercury | 88 days |
| Venus | 225 days |
| Earth | 365 days |
| Mars | 687 days |
| Jupiter | 12 years |
| Saturn | 29 years |
| Uranus | 84 years |
| Neptune | 165 years |

# CHAPTER 3

The inner planets are also the four smallest planets in our solar system.

Mars

Mercury

Earth

Venus

Sun

# The Inner Planets

The inner planets are the four planets closest to the Sun. Because they are solid like Earth and made of rock, they're called terrestrial (tuh-RES-tree-uhl) planets. These planets are surrounded by layers of gas called an atmosphere. The inner four planets were formed during the first 100 million years of the solar system's creation.

All the planets orbit around the Sun in the same direction.

Just like Earth's moon, Mercury's surface is covered with rocky craters.

# Mercury

Mercury is about 36 million mi. (58 million km) from the Sun. During the day, Mercury can get as hot as 870 °F (467 °C). But at night, the temperature can get as cold as -297 °F (-183 °C). Mercury is the smallest planet. It goes around the Sun so fast that its year is only 88 Earth days long.

# Venus

Venus is the second closest planet to the Sun. Its atmosphere is full of thick clouds which hold in heat and make it the hottest planet. These clouds reflect sunlight and make Venus shine brightly. Sometimes you can see Venus from Earth during the day. Venus is covered with huge volcanoes that spew poisonous gases.

Venus has more volcanoes than any other planet.

The clouds over Venus help to keep the heat in. Volcanoes shoot out lava, or melted rock, from deep inside Venus.

# Earth

The third planet from the Sun is Earth. Earth is the only planet in the solar system where people, plants, and animals can live. It isn't too hot or cold. Unlike other planets, Earth has lots of liquid water. On hotter planets, the water has dried up because of the Sun. On colder planets, the water may be frozen. From space, Earth looks blue because it has so much water.

**Water covers 71 percent of Earth's surface.**

The Earth travels around the Sun at a speed of 18.5 mi. (30 km) per second.

# Many Moons

Many planets in our solar system have moons. Moons orbit planets because they're pulled in by gravity. Earth's moon may have been created when something big crashed into the planet four billion years ago. Chunks of rock broke off and pulled together to form the moon. Some of the others moons may be **asteroids** but many may have formed with the planets.

**The surface of the Ubehebe Crater in Death Valley, California, looks a lot like Mars.**

# Mars

The last of the terrestrial planets is Mars. Mars is the closest planet to Earth. It's half the size of our planet. Scientists think Mars' surface may have had rivers, lakes, or oceans at one time. Now the planet looks like a dry desert. Sometimes you can see Mars in the night sky and it looks red. That's because it has a lot of iron oxide in its soil. Iron oxide is what you see on metal when it gets rusty.

Mars is often called the Red Planet.

Since the 1960s, several spacecraft have been sent to explore Mars. In 2004, two vehicles called *Spirit* and *Opportunity* landed in different places on Mars to take pictures and study its rocks and surface.

Saturn

Uranus

Jupiter

Neptune

The rings around Saturn have been observed for many years. More recently, scientists have discovered faint rings around Uranus and Jupiter as well.

# CHAPTER 4

# The Outer Planets

The four outer planets are called the Jovian (JOH-vee-uhn) Planets. The name comes from the first planet, Jupiter, or *Jove* in Latin. Jupiter was the king of the ancient Roman gods. The Jovian planets may have a core of rock and ice, but their outer layers are made of gas. That's why they're also called gas giants.

Like Venus and Earth, Uranus and Neptune are almost the same size.

# Jupiter

Jupiter is the largest planet in the solar system. It's so big that you could fit one thousand planet Earths inside of Jupiter. If you look at Jupiter through an **optical telescope**, you can see the Great Red Spot. This is a huge storm in Jupiter's atmosphere that's much larger than Earth. The storm has been there for hundreds of years.

The Great Red Spot is easy to find on Jupiter. Io, Europa, Ganymede, and Callisto are Jupiter's four largest moons.

24

*Cassini* was the first spacecraft to explore Saturn's system of rings and moons from orbit. It spent seven years traveling to the planet. The colors in the small picture show Saturn's rings more clearly.

# Saturn

Saturn is the second largest planet. All of the gas giants have rings made of ice and rock, but Saturn has the biggest rings. They are up to 175,000 mi. (282,000 km) wide but are only 3,200 feet (more than 975 meters) thick. The winds around Saturn can reach more than 1,600 ft. (500 m) per second!

# Uranus

Like the other Jovian planets, Uranus doesn't have a solid surface. It's mostly made of gas. If you tried to stand on Uranus, you would fall through layers of thick clouds and gases. Uranus doesn't **rotate** like the other planets do. It spins on its side. When one **pole** is directly facing the sun, the other pole is in darkness.

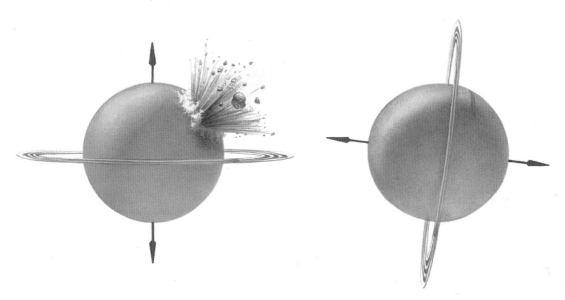

**Scientists believe that something may have crashed into Uranus when the solar system was just beginning. This caused the planet to tilt on its side.**

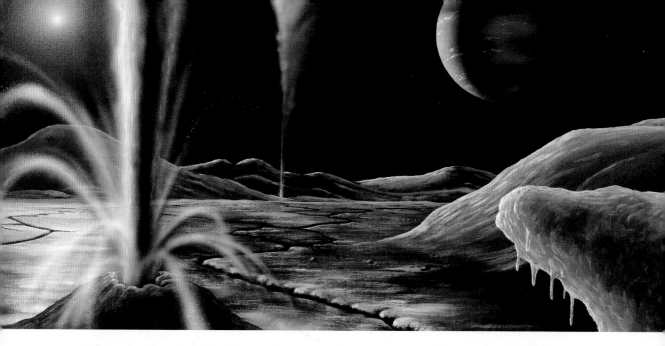

**Triton is Neptune's biggest moon. Geysers spew icy material like slush upward more than 5 mi. (8 km) and temperatures are as low as –353 °F (–214 °C).**

# Neptune

Neptune is the farthest planet from the Sun and the coldest in the solar system. Over 150 years ago, scientists noticed that something was "tugging" on Uranus and began a search for another planet. Using math, they figured out where the planet should be and then used a telescope to find it in 1846.

A cloud of dust and gas in space is called a nebula. The Orion Nebula is pictured. Newborn stars can form in the clouds of a nebula.

## 3. All Systems Go

Not all of the gas and dust in a cloud becomes a star. Sometimes extra gas and dust join together and form planets and other objects. These objects orbit the new star and become a solar system like ours.

# The Birth of a Star

How did our Sun get here? By studying older and younger stars in space, scientists think that our solar system was created 4.6 billion years ago. This was when our Sun, a star, was born.

## 1. Clouds of Dust

Most of space is filled with gas and dust. Gravity causes the gas and dust to clump together into giant clouds.

## 2. In a Spin

Gravity pulls the gas and dust towards the center of the cloud. This makes the gas and dust spin and stick together. It gets hotter, too. When enough hot gas and dust has collected in the center, the cloud begins to burn. This makes a star.

29

Pluto's moon, Charon, is half
the size of Pluto. They are locked
in the same orbit. That is why
Pluto-Charon is often called
a double planet.

# CHAPTER 5

# Not Just Planets

What else is in the solar system? There is a ring of small icy objects that orbits the Sun beyond Neptune. Pluto is located in this area and when it was discovered in 1930, it was originally called a planet. Then in 2006, **astronomers** discovered other objects bigger than Pluto and put them and Pluto into a new category called **dwarf planets**.

Pluto's three moons are Hydra, Nix, and Charon.

# Meteoroids and Asteroids

Meteoroids are bits of rock and metal passing through the solar system. They can be as small as a grain of sand or as big as a boulder. Sometimes meteoroids are pulled into a planet by gravity. A meteoroid falling toward Earth usually burns up in the atmosphere. The streak of light it makes in the sky is called a **meteor**. Meteors are sometimes called shooting stars because that's what they look like. A meteoroid that doesn't burn up entirely, but reaches the ground is called a meteorite.

Meteors

Meterorite hitting Earth

A meteoroid becomes a meteor once it passes into Earth's atmosphere.

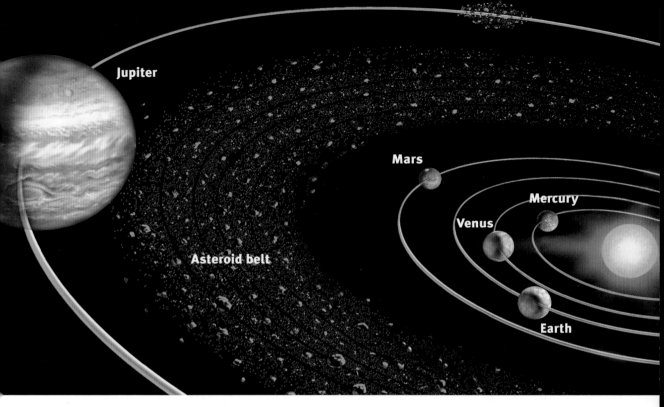

**The largest known asteroid is Ceres which is about a quarter of the size of our moon.**

Asteroids are chunks of space rock at least 0.6 mi. (1 km) wide. Most asteroids in the solar system orbit between Mars and Jupiter. They make up the asteroid belt. Some asteroids orbit close to or even cross the orbits of planets. Scientists can study asteroids to learn what the early solar system was like.

# Comets

Comets are chunks of rock, dust, and ice. A comet may only pass our solar system once

**In 1997, Comet Hale-Bopp could be seen very clearly in the night sky.**

and then return to space. Other comets may actually orbit the Sun. Some return every few years—or after a few thousand! Away from the Sun, a comet is mostly frozen. But when it gets near the Sun's heat, the ice gets very foggy and the Sun's wind pushes the fog into a long tail. Gases are pushed away from the Sun while dust particles drift back along the orbit.

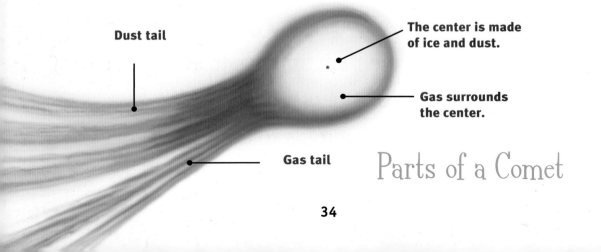

Dust tail

The center is made of ice and dust.

Gas surrounds the center.

Gas tail

Parts of a Comet

34

# The Outer Reaches

The Kuiper (KY-pur) Belt is the next part of the solar system after Neptune. It's filled with billions of chunks of frozen gas and water. Like the planets, they also orbit the Sun. But Kuiper Belt objects are much, much smaller. Dwarf planets, like Pluto, are also found in the Kuiper Belt.

The *New Horizons* spacecraft is making a one-way journey to and through the Kuiper Belt.

**Signals from the *New Horizons* spacecraft will take nearly six hours to reach Earth from Pluto.**

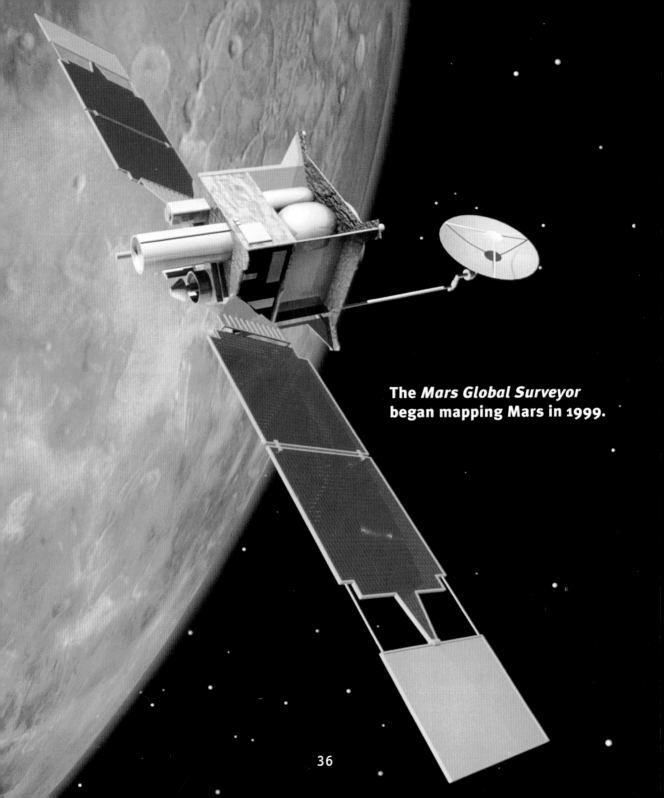

The *Mars Global Surveyor* began mapping Mars in 1999.

# CHAPTER 6

# Exploring the Solar System

People have studied the skies for thousands of years. But most of what we know about space has been discovered in the last century. Telescopes and spacecraft have helped us explore what's really out there in our solar system.

It takes about seven months to travel to Mars by spacecraft.

# Telescopes

The first telescope was invented in the 1600s. Telescopes use glass lenses and mirrors to make distant objects look bigger. Before telescopes, scientists could only look at the night sky with their eyes. Telescopes helped them find objects that didn't shine brightly. Today, large telescopes allow scientists to see farther into space.

In 1931, a man named Karl Jansky made a big discovery. He found that some objects in space gave off invisible radio waves. Until then, astronomers could only see things that gave off light.

## History of the Telescope

**1610**
Galileo uses a telescope to find four new moons around Jupiter.

**1668**
Scientist Isaac Newton builds the first reflecting telescope.

**Arecibo Observatory in Puerto Rico is the world's single largest radio telescope. Its dish is 1,000 ft. (305 m) wide.**

Scientists began building radio telescopes to study other objects in space. Today, there are telescopes that pick up other kinds of invisible energy, such as X-rays and ultraviolet and gamma rays.

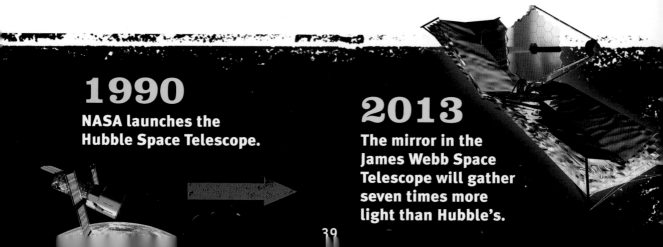

# 1990
**NASA launches the Hubble Space Telescope.**

# 2013
**The mirror in the James Webb Space Telescope will gather seven times more light than Hubble's.**

# Space Telescopes

Space telescopes orbit Earth outside its atmosphere. In 1990, the Hubble Space Telescope (HST) was the first major optical telescope ever launched. In addition to Hubble, other types of space telescopes take pictures of objects in the universe. In 2013, the James Webb Space Telescope (JWST) is scheduled to launch. It senses invisible infrared energy. JWST will help scientists learn more about other solar systems and planets deep in space.

The Hubble Space Telescope was named after Edwin P. Hubble, an American astronomer.

# Ships in Space

Since the 1960s, spacecraft have been sent to explore our solar system and beyond. We have sent robots to land on Mars. We have launched spacecraft to fly by Jupiter, Saturn, Uranus, and Neptune. Spacecraft are very useful because they can take close-up pictures. They also send information back to scientists on Earth. The spacecraft *New Horizons* was launched in 2006. It is expected to reach Pluto in 2015. After Pluto, it will continue on to explore the Kuiper Belt.

*New Horizons* **spacecraft's path to Pluto**

New Horizons

Pluto

New Horizons

Jupiter

New Horizons

Earth

# Is There Life Out There?

We know that Earth is the only planet in the solar system that has animals and plants. But scientists wonder if there might be life on other planets. Robots on Mars are testing the soil to look for evidence of past life. Some moons of Jupiter and Saturn may have liquid oceans below thick layers of ice. There could be simple life there, too! ★

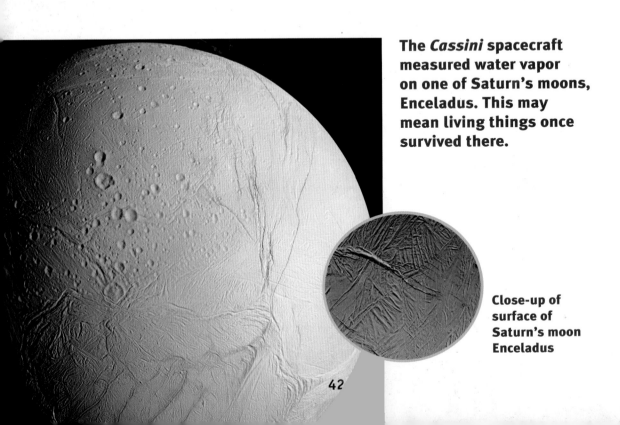

The *Cassini* spacecraft measured water vapor on one of Saturn's moons, Enceladus. This may mean living things once survived there.

Close-up of surface of Saturn's moon Enceladus

# True Statistics

**Hottest planet:** Venus, more than 880 °F (470 °C)

**Temperature at the Sun's center:** 27 million °F (15 million °C)

**Biggest moon in the solar system:** Ganymede (GAN-uh-meed), a moon of Jupiter

**Distance from the Sun to Neptune:** About 2.8 billion mi. (4.5 billion km)

**Biggest volcano in the solar system:** Olympus Mons on Mars, almost 17 mi. (27 km) high

**Number of counted asteroids in the asteroid belt:** More than 90,000

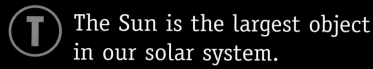

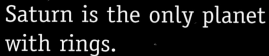

**T** The Sun is the largest object in our solar system.

**F** Saturn is the only planet with rings.

# Resources

## Books

Aguilar, David A. *Planets, Stars, and Galaxies: A Visual Encyclopedia of Our Universe.* Washington, D.C.: National Geographic Society, 2007.

Croswell, Ken. *Ten Worlds: Everything That Orbits the Sun.* Honesdale, PA: Boyds Mills Press, 2007.

Mitton, Jacqueline and Simon Mitton. *Scholastic Encyclopedia of Space.* New York: Scholastic, 1999.

Simon, Seymour. *Destination: Space.* New York: HarperCollins Publishers, 2006.

Sobel, Dava. *Planets.* New York: Viking, 2005.

Wright, Kenneth. *Scholastic Atlas of Space.* New York: Scholastic, 2005.

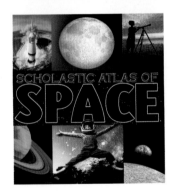

# Organizations and Web Sites

## HubbleSite Gallery
www.hubblesite.org/gallery
View pictures taken by the Hubble Space Telescope.

## NASA: Solar System Exploration
http://solarsystem.nasa.gov/kids/index.cfm
Learn about the solar system and the U.S. space program.

## Tourist Information Directory
www.touristinformationdirectory.com/Planetarium/Science_Center_Observatory_planetariums_US.htm
Visit this site to find places throughout the United States where you can learn about the solar system.

# Places to Visit

## Rose Center for Earth and Space
American Museum of Natural History
Central Park West at 79th St.
New York, NY 10024
(212) 769 5100
www.amnh.org/rose
See what the solar system looks like from space.

## Smithsonian National Air and Space Museum
Independence Ave. at 6th St., SW
Washington, DC 20560
(202) 633 1000
www.nasm.si.edu
View spacecraft that have traveled to the moon.

# Important Words

**asteroids** (AS-tuh-roids) – large pieces of rock that orbit the Sun

**astronomers** (uh-STRON-uh-muhrs) – scientists who study objects in space

**comets** – large chunks of rock and ice that travel around the Sun

**dwarf planets** – bodies in the solar system that orbit the Sun, have a constant (nearly round) shape, and are not moons. Pluto is a dwarf planet.

**gravity** – a force that pulls two objects together

**meteor** – the trail of light made by a meteoroid entering Earth's atmosphere

**meteoroids** (MEE-tee-ur-roids) – small pieces of rock or metal in space

**optical telescope** – an instrument that uses glass lenses and mirrors to study objects in space

**orbits** – the path taken by one body circling another body

**pole** – one of two opposite points on the surface of a spinning planet

**rotate** – to turn about an axis or center

# Index

Page numbers in **bold** indicate illustrations

# About the Author

Howard K. Trammel writes fiction and nonfiction books for both children and adults. His topics range from science and history to how to raise teenagers. At 11 years old, Mr. Trammel stayed up late to watch the first moonwalk on television. Although he's never traveled in space himself, Mr. Trammel has lived in the solar system his entire life.

DISCARD

6/10